PINTEREST
for You and
Your Business

Illustrated Basics of Pinterest as a Social Network, Tips and Strategies to Increase Your Visibility and Build Your Brand

Mark Sheppard

DISCLAIMER

Disclaimer and Terms of Use: Effort has been made to ensure that the information in this book is accurate and complete. However, the author and the publisher do not warrant the accuracy of the information, text, and graphics contained within the book due to the rapidly changing nature of science, research, known and unknown facts and internet. The Author and the publisher do not hold any responsibility for errors, omissions or contrary interprctation of the subject matter herein. This book is presented solely for motivational and informational purposes

CONTENTS

DISCLAIMER _____ 3

CONTENTS _____ 5

INTRODUCTION _____ 7

WELCOME TO PINTEREST! _____ 13

An organized bulletin board – make that boards _____ 14

A Few "Pinteresting" Stats _____ 15

HOW TO USE PINTEREST _____ 16

Opening Your Account _____ 16

Pinning any Image from any Website_____ 19

An Alternate Route_____ 20

Creating a Board _____ 22

Use this Window to Create a New Board _____ 23

What? Pinning videos? Not me! _____ 25

Step-By-Step Instructions to Video Pinning _____ 26

Viewing and Reviewing Your Pinterest Boards_____ 28

Deleting or Editing Your Boards_____ 29

INTERERACTING WITH THE PINTEREST COMMUNITY ___ 31

Who Should You Follow? _____ 32

Repinning: A New Internet Term_____ 34

How to "Like" a Pin _____ 35

Commenting on an Image _____ 37

Reviewing your Comments _____ 37

Second Thoughts About What You Said? _____ 38

7 TIPS TO USING PINTEREST _____39

Pinterest Tip #1: Seeing the Source of a Pin _____39

Pinterest Tip #2: Learn the shortcut to creating a caption ___41

Pinterest Tip #3: Send a Private Message via Pinterest_____41

Pinterest Tip #4: Seek out those with like minds. _____42

Pinterest Tip #5: Deleting specific search topics_____43

Pinterest Tip #6: Pinning a personal photo to the site _____43

Pinterest Tip #7: Use the Help Center _____45

TO MARKET, TO MARKET WITH PINTEREST _____47

1. Tagging others in your pins _____48

2. Create a Pinterest-Based Online Catalogue _____49

3. Include an active link to your web site in your product description._____49

4. Get your site verified._____50

5. By all means, keep in active contact with individuals in the Pinterest community._____52

6. Avoid flooding your boards with self-promotion _____52

7. Sponsor a Pinterest Contest _____53

CONCLUSION _____55

INTRODUCTION

Welcome to the Age of Social Media!

Yes, I know it's been a part of our lives for quite a while now. And many of us have tried as hard as we can to ignore it. However, the tighter you close your eyes and try to ignore social media, the closer you seem to be finding it!

First, there was myspace, then Facebook. After that there seemed, to the casual eye at least, a flood of smaller and some major social media sites, including Instagram, snapchat, and Twitter to name just a few.

Of course, don't forget Pinterest. Of all the sites, this is the one that is nearly exclusively devoted to the collection, long-term display and sharing of pictures, photos, and graphics of all kinds. If you had to choose one social media site to learn about and join, this just might be the one.

You're interested, but maybe you aren't quite sure how it works. If only you could find some solid information about it. That's where this guide comes in! It's aimed at those of us who never claimed to be either tech savvy or have a great deal of experienced navigating the social media sites.

This book, however, is aimed at the individual who wants to learn more. It's written for the person who's curious and even eager to make up for lost time and begin to become more active on the web and wants to start with Pinterest.

Your curiosity, though, may go a bit deeper. Sure, you know enough to realize that Pinterest is a rapidly growing social media site, but what do you really know about social media? That's why we're going to start by explaining a little about what people mean when talk about "social media."

Social media is the now commonly used term for interactive web sites in which individuals can not only post information about what's going on in their lives – think something akin to an electronic diary of sorts – and other people can respond to them. Many of us use social media everyday and don't even think about it.

Facebook is probably the first site like this comes to mind. You may already be one of the millions of individuals avidly using it. You post your "profile," information you'd like others to know about your background. Then you begin to post short informational bursts on what is called your "wall."

Other social media sites include Snapchat, blogs that encourage comments, Instagram, and Twitter to name just a small fraction.

There's really no way around it. Social media is the future of communication. It might not be as romantic as the Civil War soldier writing to his true love in his own handwriting from the battlefield, but it's that equivalent for today and moving forward.

It nonetheless has helped millions of families, husbands, wives, children, mothers and fathers keep in touch, sometimes through video chats over many miles. Even the staunchest of social media critics has to admit that.

The site we're talking about in this book may not provide any service quite that essential, but it's a fun and useful way to interact with others on the web.

Pinterest does exactly this, only with one distinctive difference. Think of this site as an electronic bulletin board. You post photos of items you find on other web sites, from recipes to quotes with photos with them, to photos of gardening ideas and renovations.

If you've been thinking about joining the Pinterest community but aren't quite sure what it entails or how to use to best serve your needs, I'll take you through the process from signing up to repinning other people's posts.

The following are just a few of the aspects of this popular site you'll learn how to:

1. To join the site and build a profile
2. Pin graphics to your board
3. Create categories of pins for different topics, such as recipes, home furnishings, books and more!
4. "Repinning" of other persons' original pins
5. Editing your boards
6. "Liking" boards to show support to others

Wait, there's more!

This guide will also show you how you can take Pinterest with you wherever you go. You can now download applications that allow you to access this growing social media site not only on your computer, but also on your cell phone, tablet, laptop, and iPad.

Next, are you thinking about starting a business?

If you are or are already running one, you'll discover that because of the site's unique demographics, it's an effective method of promoting your products and services.

If you haven't thought about it before, you may want to consider using it as a part of your overall marketing strategy. If that's the case, there's a chapter devoted entirely to it.

I've even devoted an entire chapter to Pinterest tips – suggestions on how to use this site to maximize the fun and excite and lessen the potential for frustration.

Are you ready to begin to learn one of the hottest social media sites around? Let's get started!

WELCOME TO PINTEREST!

What is it?

The best way to describe Pinterest is to compare it to a bulletin board. It's a display of images with captions built on electronic boards divided into a variety of categories. Individuals display items they love, recipes they'd like to refer back to, even covers of books they've either read or are planning to read.

Remember when you were a kid and your mother used to put all your artwork on the refrigerator? Think of Pinterest as the "refrigerator" of the internet. It's where people worldwide show off whatever images they're proud of.

More than that, though, it's a social media site, which means that not only can you display items you've found from other web sites, but also that others can comment on your items. They can even "re-pin" them and place them on their own accounts, just as you can do with whatever's on their boards.

That's what millions of people worldwide are already doing. Actually, Pinterest has grown into more than that. Just like any other social media site, businesses find it exceedingly useful as one way to market their goods and services. So, when you're first browsing the site, don't be surprised to uncover images of items that just might be for sale.

An organized bulletin board – make that boards

Your Pinterest account is more than one bulletin board. It's a multitude of boards, all of which can be organized into categories at your own discretion. You can have as many boards with images pinned to them as you wish. Not only that, but it's totally up to you how to label them.

If you're at a loss when you initially sign on to the site for possible categories you want to use, browse the site to see the topics other individuals are pinning. This gives you an idea of how you may want to organize your boards.

Not to worry, though, if you decide to change your mind and re-organize your boards and change topics. It's easy enough to do! I'll show how to do that in an upcoming chapter.

The developers of Pinterest couldn't have made easier for you to pin your interests to your new bulletin boards. The bottom line is that you don't have to leave the site on which you found the image and move over to Pinterest in order to post it. It's as simple as using the Pinterest application logo that shows up on each image once you load it.

A Few "Pinteresting" Stats

When you make the decision to become part of the community, you might be interested in knowing that you'll become part of a 70-million member community. While that might not impress you if your interest in the site is purely for staying in contact with family and friends, you may find it more impressive if you're considering it as part of your marketing platform for your business.

When you join Pinterest, you are joining a group that is largely based with female users. It's estimated that at least 80% and as much as 90% of the users are women, depending on which sources you read.

Here's another statistic that's especially engaging if you decide to market any product on the site. The average U.S. woman on Pinterest has 67 followers. What does that mean to you as a marketer? For starters, if you can just engage one woman to post one of your products, you have the potential of reaching 67 other women who'll be exposed to that post!

HOW TO USE PINTEREST

So you've decided you want to join the Pinterest community. Well, you've come to the right place. This chapter walks you through the steps of using the site from creating an account to actually pinning and repinning posts.

Since this book is aimed at beginners, I'm going to assume that you know absolutely nothing about the site. I offer my apologies to those of you who may have a bit of exposure to Pinterest and are already logged in. You may find the beginning section of this chapter a bit tedious.

For everybody else, let's get started!

Opening Your Account

If you've never visited Pinterest before, your first step is to open an account.

The site provides you with three ways of opening an account. You can open one either through your existing Facebook or Twitter accounts, or you can open it through your primary email account. For the moment, let's assume you either have no other social media accounts, or you prefer to open it with your email address.

In order to access Pinterest initially and open an account, you can type the word "Pinterest" in your browser and allow it to guide you to the proper page. If you'd like, though, you may want to enter the following address into your browser directly: www.pinterest.com.

You'll provide them with your email address, create a password that you know you can remember and others would have a tough time guessing, and click the button that says "Sign up."

There are several advantages to signing up with just your email address, not the least of which is that it keeps your Pinterest account separate from the other two. If, at a later date, you'd like to connect Pinterest to either Facebook, Twitter, or both, you can still do so.

From here, the site takes you to the "Create Your Account" page. Simply follow the form the site offers. It's all self-explanatory. It will ask you to provide your email address, your password for Pinterest, and your first and last names.

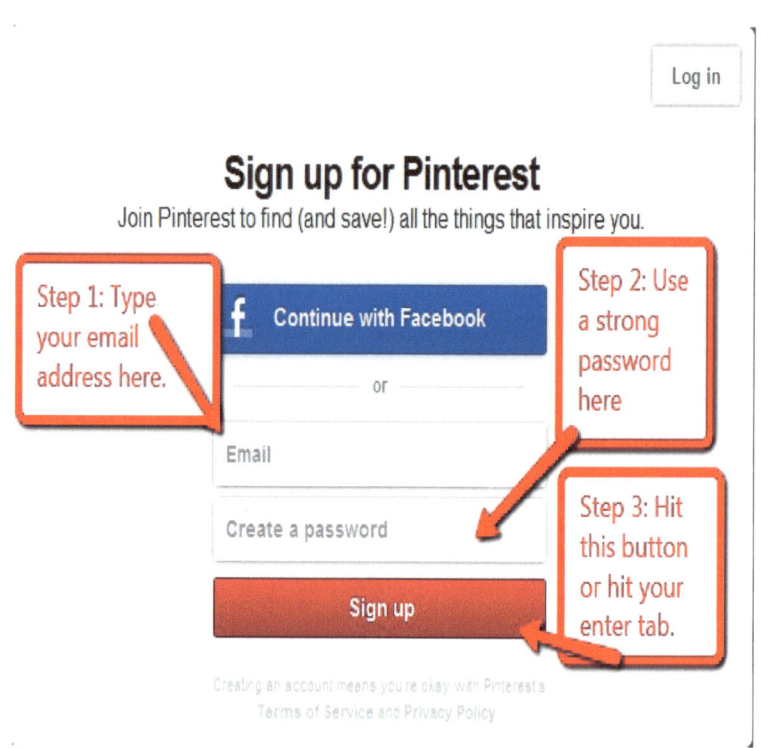

If you're using Pinterest as a personal social media tool, you'll undoubtedly want to use your first and last name. Many individuals with businesses may prefer to open an account under their business name. If that's the case with you, think about opening a business account instead. You can reach that page through this URL:http://business.pinterest.com/. (We'll talk more about how to get the most mileage out of marketing with Pinterest later in the book.)

Pinning any Image from any Website

Once you've done that, you can then click on the "Create Account" button. Now you have your own account and can browse the site a bit! It's time now to install what in Pinterest jargon is called a "bookmarklet." This allows you to pin any image from any web site. All this requires is:

1. You go to this page on the site: http://www.pinterest.com/about/goodies.

2. At the top of this page, you can't miss a large red button that reads "Pin It." Place your cursor over this and drag it to the bookmarks bar in your browser if you're using either Chrome or Mozilla Firefox.

Or:

1. If you're using Windows Explorer to reach the web, the process is a bit different. You're still going to start from the page I cited in Step One above, but now you're going to right click your mouse on this same item.

2. Then you'll choose an option that says, "Add to Favorites."

3. A window appears that asks where you'd like to add this icon. Choose "Favorites" from this drop-list.

4. Then click "Add."

And that's all there is to it! You're ready to become an active member of the Pinterest community. You can use this icon anytime you want to add a graphic to one of your boards!

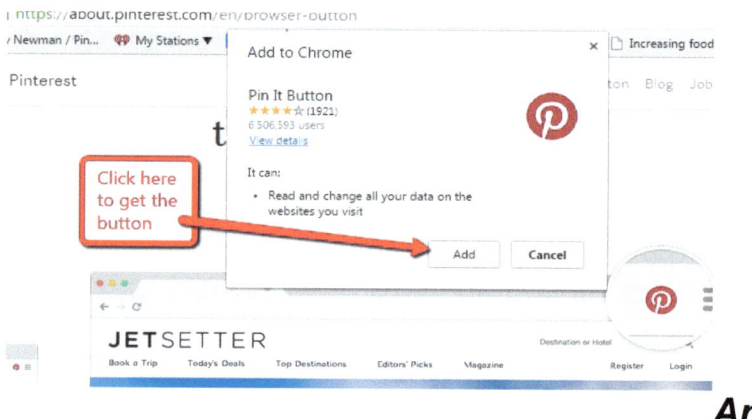

An

Alternate Route

While that's one way to place items to your site, there's a second very effective way to post. It's supplied as a courtesy for you. Quite frankly, it also helps the web site with its promotions, publicity, and popularity when web sites provide it.

Remember that "Pinit" icon we added to your browser task bar? It's right next to where the URL of the web site is displayed. When you find this and choose to use this route, you begin by clicking on it.

1. A new window pops up showing you the photos on that web site.

2. Simply choose the image you want and what board you'd like it on.

3. You'll then have the opportunity to enter a brief description or a comment.

4. The only other decision you need to make is if you want to share it on your Facebook and Twitter accounts as well.

5. Your final step, of course, is to "Pin It."

6. The "success window" now appears, confirming that you were indeed successful in completing the pinning.

7. It is also at this point you can choose which board you would like to pin it on.

Creating a Board

By definition, just being a member of the Pinterest community gives you one "bulletin" board. There'll come a time, and it will come much quicker than you think, that you'll want to organize your pins in some manner. The type of organization you use, of course, is totally up to you.

There are also several different ways to accomplish this. Every time you open your Pinterest account, you'll immediately land on the page on which you get a glimpse of some of the images of those you're following. In order to get to your page of boards, simply click on your name. You'll find this on the top upper right corner of the page.

The way to give yourself a second (and third) board is by clicking on the "Add+" link at the top of your page. This summons a new window. You can either create a new pin or an entirely new board from here. Right now you'll select the new board option. Once you've done that, the window prompts you to put the information of your choice on it in order identify it.

Use this Window to Create a New Board

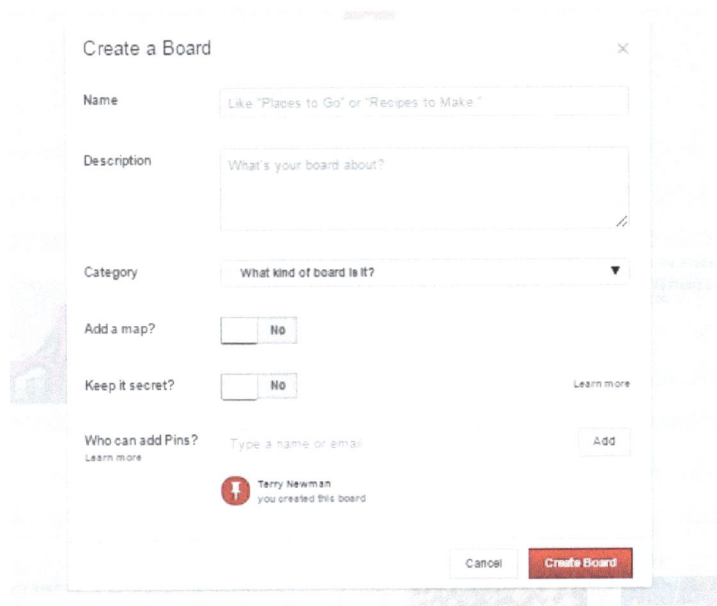

You'll definitely want to provide your second board with a name – something different from your first, of course. Obviously, its name will reflect the subject manner you'll be filing into it. You'll also be prompted to select from several categories just in case you can't come up with a good title yourself.

You have one option left before you navigate away from this window. That's whether you want the public to be able to view this board or if you would rather keep it private so that only you can review it. If you keep it for your personal viewing only, Pinterest refers to it as a "secret board."

There's a catch here, though. Pinterest only allows you to create three secret boards per account. Think about it carefully before you actually click on this option. Only three, you may think. But really, the entire concept behind the site is to form a community in which persons share common interests with others. Having too many secret boards violates the entire spirit of the site.

You can't change a board that the public is currently viewing to a private or "secret" board. You can, however, convert the secret board into one that all members of the Pinterest public can view. Keep in mind though the rules for public Pinterest boards now apply to this board as well; namely, this board cannot revert back to a secret board. Really, it's not as complicated as it sounds.

It all can be sums up in two simple rules: 1.) Once a public board, always a public board, and 2.) only three secret boards per account at any given time. If you convert a secret board to public, it can't go back to being secret. If you keep this in your mind, you'll be fine!

You may believe at this point you've completed everything there is to do and you can navigate away. There's still one more task to take care of: that of giving another individual, if you wish, the ability to pin to this board.

Why would you even want someone to be able to do it? Think about it for a moment. It's a great way to share a photo with a family member. Pin up a cute saying that you know that your daughter might enjoy. Invite your parents or other members of your family. Invite your closest friends. The more, the merrier!

If you would like another person to pin to your board, then type, where prompted to, the first and last names of that person. You'll be shown the people on the site with that name. Once you find the person, you click onto the button marked, "Invite." The magic of cyberspace sees to it that they get the information.

Your last step in all of this though is to then hit the button marked "Create Board." Poof! You now have an additional board.

What? Pinning videos? Not me!

Yes, you. You've conquered the pinning of photos. It really is as simple as it appears. But guess what? You've now watched a great video that you wish you could share with others.

This is one of the more exciting aspects of this site, which is currently being used by everyone from writers to business executives to life coaches.

The ideas here are practically unlimited. If your hobby is crafting, then you can add a tutorial video on your boards to help others craft the same creations you did. If you're into music or a musician yourself, you can pin music videos on your boards.

Don't have any videos yourself, but found one on another board you'd like to repin? That's easy enough to do. And yes, by the way, that play button in the middle of the image does indicate it's already been pinned.

Step-By-Step Instructions to Video Pinning

1. Click the "add" button at the top of the page on which the video is located. This, brings up the "add" window.

2. Now click on the "Add a pin" icon. This asks you for the URL address of the video. This is the page in the browser on which the video is located.

3. Go back to the page where the video is located. Left click in the address space. Right click and choose "copy." This copies the address. Go back to Pinterest where the URL address has been requested. Right click in that space and choose "paste." The address is entered! Once you enter this you'll be able to actually view the video you would like to pin to your board.

4. Decide which board you'd like to pin it to and then enter a brief description of it.

5. Just like with photos, you always have the option of sharing it at the same moment you pin it to your board through Facebook or Twitter.

Or

You can use the bookmarklet on your web browser to add it to your board. When you click this button, you'll be calling up a new window. It's here you choose the video you wish to pin.

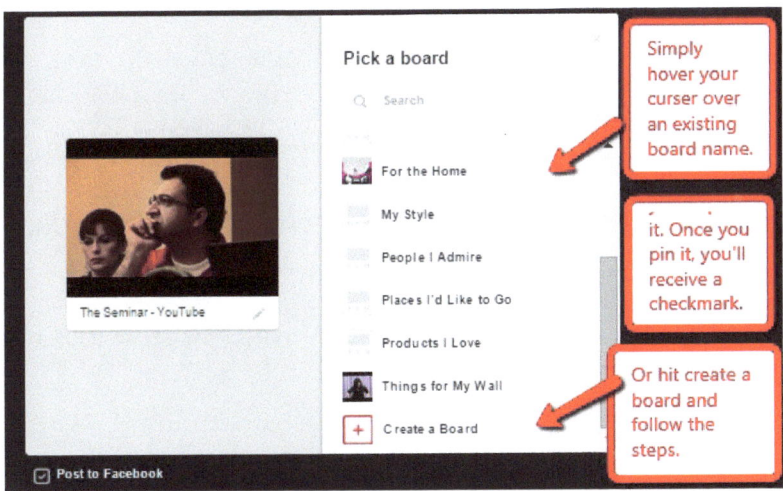

Viewing and Reviewing Your Pinterest Boards

Well, it only makes sense. You're pinning these images up so you can go back and view them at a later date. Many individuals use Pinterest as a cyber recipe book, pinning them onto this web site so that they're all in one place. They may not have yet tried it, having just stumbled across it, but they want to "store" it in a convenient location for future use.

Others have a board with all their dreams and visions for the future. They'll pin items up precisely so that they can come back look at them and either daydream or envision their goals into reality.

Whatever your reason for pinning these photos, chances are you'll want to revisit them on occasion.

To review what you've already placed on your boards, simply click or hover over your name. You'll find that the "Boards" menu appears. It should come as no surprise that this is where you can check out your own boards.

It will also show you a few statistics about your collection. For example, it'll show you how many pins or images you have on each board. It'll also show you the last four images you pinned on these boards. You can also view the cover image for each category if you added one.

Deleting or Editing Your Boards

Hmm. Let's say you've pinned that delicious-looking recipe on a board. The recipe, however, turned out to be, well, disappointing at best. Now that you know that, you'll never use it again. You'd really like to delete this recipe and pretend the whole disaster never happened. Or are you stuck looking at this deceptive recipe forever?

You can remove it as well as any other image you may not want on your board anymore. In fact you can even delete an entire board if you'd like. Once again, it's far easier than you thought possible.

Let's start by editing an existing board. Simply click on the board you'd like to make the make the changes to. As you do this, you'll see a button appear that's labeled "Edit Board." Clicking on it will open it and will allow you to do just that.

Go to the "Options" page where it will allow you edit the title, description, and category of the board. You can also change the name of the individual who can pin to this board, if you so desire.

Once you've made your changes, you'll just have to hit "Save Settings." Your board is now edited.

If you want, you can edit any of the images on this board while you're in there. You do this by clicking on the image. Here you can change the description or anything else about the image. You can even delete the photo here.

While you're here, you're also given the option of actually deleting the entire board. You've probably already found it. It's labeled "Delete Board," and if you haven't noticed it yet, it's at the top of the page on the right side. Simply click this. Before the board is actually deleted, Pinterest pops up with a confirmation alert. It just wants to be sure that you purposely hit that button. If you did, and you really do want to delete it, just confirm your decision. And that board, as they say, is history.

Now that you've conquered the basics of your "private domain" in the Pinterest community, let's extend your reach a bit. It's time to wander around the community some. When you're ready, follow me around the Pinterest "town."

INTERERACTING WITH THE PINTEREST COMMUNITY

Part of the fun of being an active member of the Pinterest site is the effort the website founders have gone to in order to make you feel like you belong to a "real community." This makes this site unique. If you already belong to Facebook, you know that in order to interact with someone, that person needs to agree.

On Pinterest, you can use more passive means to interact with others by doing something the site calls "following." This means that you'll be privy to what they pin. If you are, that means when you open your account, one of the first things you'll see are the boards of those you've tagged to "follow."

The bottom line in this is, unlike some other sites, you don't need them to agree. There's no "friending" or "unfriending" like on Facebook.

Who Should You Follow?

Perhaps you've been browsing and noticed someone has some great pictures of "dream homes," or super gluten-free recipes. You may want to follow them.

Many individuals purposely seek out family, friends, or contacts from other sites to follow. Who do you want to follow? Once you've decided who, here are the steps you need to follow to make it happen.

Go to one of their recent pins, and click your mouse on their name. This is located under the object pinned. You've just opened the pinner's page. Here you can view all of their pins and categories of boards.

You have a choice between following only select topics or all of the boards. If you decide to follow the entire collection, all you need to do is to choose the "Follow All" button located at the top of the page.

You're not quite done, though. Your final steps include clicking on your name that's at the top of this page as well as your profile. This is a double check to make sure you're now following. In fact, this latter page shows you all the individuals you're currently following.

Perhaps, though, you're not interested in following all of their boards. There's only one topic that interests you. Perhaps this is a board of gluten-free recipes, but all the other boards aren't of any interest to you.

In that case, you find the category of the board you would like to follow. Click on the board and then click on the "Follow" button. This toward the top of the page. You'll know that you're following them because as soon as you click on it, the button turns gray, and then simply says "Unfollow."

If you're not exactly comfortable taking the computer's word the transaction took place. When you return to your profile page you can confirm it.

Here's where some individuals get a bit confused. You're looking at a list of individuals you're already following, yet you still see an active "Follow" button asking you to choose it. This indicates you're only following one or two of their boards, not their entire collection.

Should you change your mind later and would like to follow their entire collection, choose this button.

Repinning: A New Internet Term

Doesn't it seem as if with every new web site, another new "cyber word" is invented? When we entered the Facebook age of the internet it was "unfriend," to indicate that you had changed your mind, and you didn't want that individual to see your posts any more.

Now with Pinterest we have made fashionable the term "repin." Sure, some of us used this word before, but in totally different contexts. Now you say the word "repin" and just about everyone knows what you mean.

It's when you find a picture on Pinterest you like and choose to share it with your followers. You take that particular image and put it on one of your boards. That's what meant by repinning. If you've taken any time on this site as we've been learning it, then you know it happens quite a bit.

By the way, if you really like the image or it works well on more than one board in your account, feel free to post it to as many of your own boards as you like. You'll eventually want to do it – we all do. Here is all you need to know. Take your cursor and hover it over the image. Within seconds, you'll notice that you'll see three different icons, each representing one of the options you have.

They include "Repin," "Like," and "Comment." In this instance, obviously, you'll want to choose the "Repin" choice. This brings us the "repin window." A drop-down box appears at this time. It allows you to place this image on a board you've already created or it gives you an opportunity to create a new board.

If you want to start a new board, all you need to do is to scroll down the option. Now you'll be prompted to give this new board a name. Once you've repinned this, a message that you've successfully accomplished this appears.

How to "Like" a Pin

In the paragraphs above, three options popped up when you went to repin an image; the repin, as well as a "Like" button and a "Comment" button. You can show your appreciation of the image without pinning it to your board. That would be with the "Like" button.

There could be any number of reasons why you would do this without repinning it to your account. If you want to like it, start as you did before, by taking your cursor and hovering the image. This time, instead of clicking on the "Repin" option, you're going to choose the "Like" button.

Just as before, the "Like" button turns grey and now reads "Unlike." Here's another new "cyber word" for you. This gives you the option at any time you like to change your mind about this particular image.

When you do this, you're only showing your public appreciation for this image on Pinterest site alone. There is a way that you can like this image so your appreciation also appears on Facebook.

Click on the image to have it fill the entire page. Look to the right side of the photo. That's where a "Like" button is that's linked to the Facebook site. Choose this "Like" button, and you'll then be asked to log in to Facebook. If you've liked more than one image, you'll be able to find the list of the images you've just liked on your profile menu.

You can see this by hovering your cursor over your name. This brings up a menu that includes a choice called (creatively enough) "Likes." You'll click on this option shows all of the photos -you've liked.

Commenting on an Image

This now brings us to that third option we saw when we first started liking photos from others. On Pinterest, you're invited to comment on any or all images you've viewed, regardless of whose account it's on.

Once again, you'll take your cursor and hover over the image. When the "Comment" button appears, simply choose it by clicking on to it. Look directly under the graphic. This is where you're going to record your comment. When you're finished, click on the "Comment" button a second time. This saves your remarks.

Reviewing your Comments

Let's say you want to review your comments for whatever reason. In order to do this, you'll navigate to your "Activity" page. You can get here by clicking on your name.

This again opens your profile page. You'll notice a menu bar that includes a choice of "Activity." This is exactly what you're looking for. All of your recent actions are displayed here. That, of course, includes all of your comments.

Second Thoughts About What You Said?

Have you had any second thoughts about those comments you left on one of the graphics? If you'd really like to remove those remarks, unlike email and texts sent through cyber space, you can actually do this.

Now be careful here. While you can remove it, you cannot edit it.

Once you delete the comment, you can always add another, which is just as good as editing. You can find the image through searching your activity page or by accessing the photo itself. Scroll to your comment. You'll discover an "x" next to your comment. Hit it. Poof. Your comment has disappeared.
If you don't want to say anything else about it, you're finished. However, you're also free now to replace it with another remark.

Congratulations! You now know your way around one of the hottest social media sites on the internet today. You see, it was much easier than you originally thought it would be!

While it would easy to leave you on your own at this point, I've also included a marvelous chapter providing you with tips on how to enjoy your time in the Pinterest community to the fullest.

7 TIPS TO USING PINTEREST

Now that you've got the basics done, it's time you're privy to a few of the advanced techniques, little-known tips and awesome tricks that veterans of the site may never think to tell you. You'll be surprised at how often you'll end up using them.

Pinterest Tip #1: Seeing the Source of a Pin

There may come a time when curiosity will get the better of you, and you'd really like to see where in the world that particular photo came from. It may be you'd like the image so much, you'd like to visit the web site or its original source.

Yes, you can do that! And it's much easier than you think. Of course, there's one caveat here. You can do this as long as you're viewing the original pinned document and not the "repinning" of one.

When you click on the image to view its source this is what you'll see.

This is the Pinterest board you discovered it on

This is the original source of the image. Click on this to get to the web site.

Every time someone pins something to her board, the information about its original source is attached. If you click on the original image, you'll find all the information you need about its source.

If the person who pinned the image initially took it from her personal computer, the source information would not have traveled with the pinned item. She would have had to take the time to manually insert this information. More often than not, this isn't done.

The flip side is, though, that if it's taken from anywhere from the net, it'll be visible to you.

Pinterest Tip #2: Learn the shortcut to creating a caption

Here's a cool shortcut you'll eventually want to try once you get accustomed to pinning. The best advantage of this little trick is that it allows you to pin a little faster.

When you use the "Pin it" button from your browser task bar, you are can actually highlight a portion of the original caption of the graphic. Use your discretion to choose the wording you believe is the best possible description of the object. Then when you do hit that button you have an automatic description without you having to type anything in.

Pinterest Tip #3: Send a Private Message via Pinterest

This is a relatively new aspect of the web site and not that well known by many users. The site now allows you to directly pin to individuals both inside and outside the community. In order to do this, you simply hover your cursor over the image you'd like to send.

In a bit (you may not see it immediately, so be patient), this will reveal a "send" button toward the top of the screen. Click on this and you'll be able to attach your personal message as well as who you'd like to send it to. This includes anyone you know currently on Pinterest, other social media sites, or if you'd like, you can even email the pin to your friend.

Pinterest Tip #4: Seek out those with like minds.

Remember that Pinterest was created to be an interactive community. It's a site that encourages you to communicate with others, preferably those with similar tastes.

Again, just like everything else on this site, it's really quite easy to do. Let's say you're pinning an image you really love and want to find similar photos. Go to the section called "Also on these boards." When you scroll down the site, it'll show you other boards related to yours.

This is an easy and organized way to find other boards where your image has appeared. You just might, in the process, find a new person you could follow. Many veteran users of the site say they've found some of their favorite pinners in this fashion.

Pinterest Tip #5: Deleting specific search topics

There's many reasons why you may want to clear specific searches you've performed in the recent past on Pinterest. I clear my searches regularly just out of habit. Whatever the reason, let's say you don't want a certain search topic showing up. In that case, you have the option to delete it.

To do this you start by navigating to your "Account Settings" page. To the left of your "Search History" tab, you'll find a button that reads "Clear Recent Searches." Click this button, and your most recent searches will disappear.

Search history   (Clear Recent Searches)   Remove things you've recently searched for from search suggestions

Pinterest Tip #6: Pinning a personal photo to the site

Yes, of course it's possible. Let's say you've been pinning about creative methods to create bookshelves out of unusual items. This has inspired your creativity and you've recently re-purposed an unusual item into an inspiring book shelf. You'd like to take the photo of it on your computer and upload them to a Pinterest board

It's easy to do. On every Pinterest page there's a bar at the top with the button that reads "Add." Click this. It doesn't matter actually what page you find it on. It's available on all pages. Next you click on "Upload a Pin." From there it's going to give you several choices. One of these is "Choose a File." This is the one you want to click on.

This option allows you to choose an image from your computer. The key here is to know where in your computer you've saved your photo. If you're anything like me, this is usually the most difficult part of the process. If you haven't done it already, create a new file on your desktop and label it "pictures." Inside that file, you can create more files, including one marked "Pinterest." Problem solved. You'll always know where your pics are.

After you've found your photo, select a board on which you want to place it and then give it a title. Now you're ready to click the "Pin it" button.

Pinterest Tip #7: Use the Help Center

That's right! This may seem like obvious advice, but if the truth be told, most of us shy away from areas like "Help Centers." We've been conditioned from our experience that they're far too often the "black holes" of the internet. Certainly they were created with nothing but good intentions, but they usually are not as helpful as they were intended.

In fact, I can't tell you how many "Help Centers" I've used on various web sites only to be more entangled in the steps and more confused than when I entered. This isn't so with Pinterest. You'll discover it both easy to navigate and with advice that is explicit and easy to understand.

By now, you're a proficient Pinterest user! That's great. Perhaps, though, you'd really like to take the natural power of this social media site and work it to make a bit of extra money. Or even wield its marketing power for the company you work for.

Whether you're marketing custom-crafted soap, hand-knitted scarves, or furniture, Pinterest can be an exceptional promotion and marketing platform.

In the following chapter, I provide you with only a few easy ideas of how to start using the site today to make money.

TO MARKET, TO MARKET WITH PINTEREST

It's true! The visual nature of the Pinterest community, almost by definition, make it an ideal site to market. That's what many are already doing, from individual entrepreneurs to large corporations. They're all discovering that this site has a potential buying power. It has power that largely has been overlooked and is ready to be mined.

The fact that the site has 70 million users in the States alone – an overwhelming number of them women – helps you understand why more businesses are staking an active claim on the site. And you can too!

Whether you're working part-time at a new business venture or full time in a marketing department of a large company, you're about to discover how incredibly useful the Pinterest community can be to your bottom line.

Your job right now is to change your perception of Pinterest and begin to tap its rich, nearly untouched market. Below are a few tips to get you started. As you begin to get incredible results from Pinterest, you'll be amazed at not only who is waiting to buy your product, but also at how many consumers are waiting for you.

1. Tagging others in your pins

It's a simple technique, yet it's ingenious. If you're on Facebook at all, you already know a little something about tagging. It's simply adding one or more persons who happened to be with you at the time of the event.

My sister-in-law often tags me in her pictures, even if I'm not in the photo she's uploading to Facebook. If there's a group of us playing a board game (especially if she wins), she tags everyone involved.

The theory is the same in Pinterest, but you can take it one step further to optimize the number of individuals who see that lavender scarf you're knitting and who may be thinking about birthday or Christmas gifts.

As a marketer, you'd want to tag a certain person with many followers and one who is known to re-pin material. It may take a bit of time to find these boards initially, but once you've found them, you may have just struck gold.

This isn't a technique you'll be able to use the moment you step into the community. It will require you to keep a careful eye on the boards, where you post, who's following you, and how many individuals are following your followers. Because Pinterest is so open-ended in this sense, it really can be achieved. And once you've caught on, you'll see your sales increase.

2. Create a Pinterest-Based Online Catalogue

What better place for a visual display of not only products, but your services as well? Let's all think about Christmas for a moment, the time of year when our mail boxes get clogged with catalogue after catalogue.

With the ease of loading pictures to the web – especially to Pinterest – this option really is a no-brainer. You not only put the photos of your products and services on the site, but you also add a brief description.

3. Include an active link to your web site in your product description.

This one small action represents the height of brilliance in marketing. This means with just a click of a mouse, any individual can jump over to your site, check out the product in more detail, and buy it right then and there.

It only takes a few very simple steps to do this as well. Let's start with a pin from your board. Click on it to bring the image up. It will look like the one below.

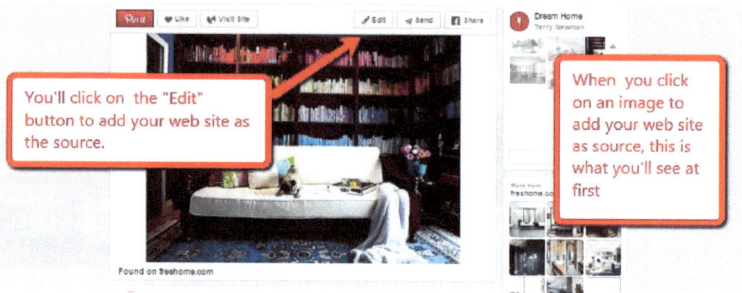

Once you click on the "Edit" button you'll get another window. It will look similar to the one below. In the area marked "source" you'll add your complete URL. Then click the "Save Changes" button.

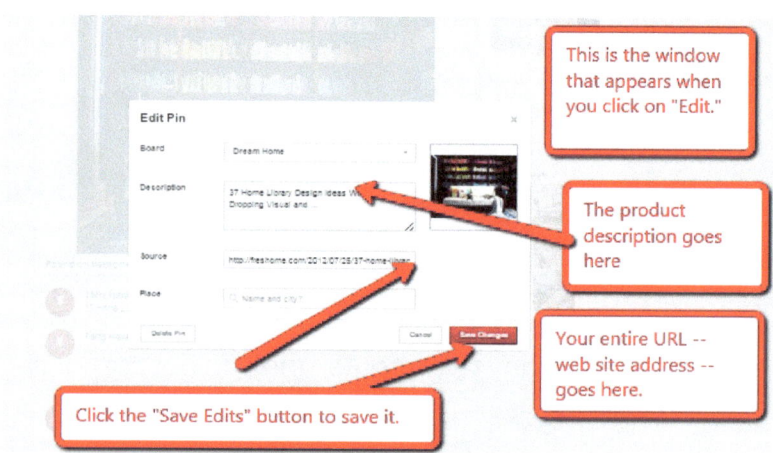

4. Get your site verified.

This is easy enough to do and creates a trusting relationship between your business and the consumer. You'll discover the easy-to-follow guidelines in the help center.

This not only protects the consumer, who now knows you're a solid company, but it also helps you because it prevents others from representing themselves as your business.

The first step is to hit the "Edit Profile" at the top right section of your home page. This window appears on your computer screen. Please sure to fill out this window completely, before hitting the verification button. The window will look like this:

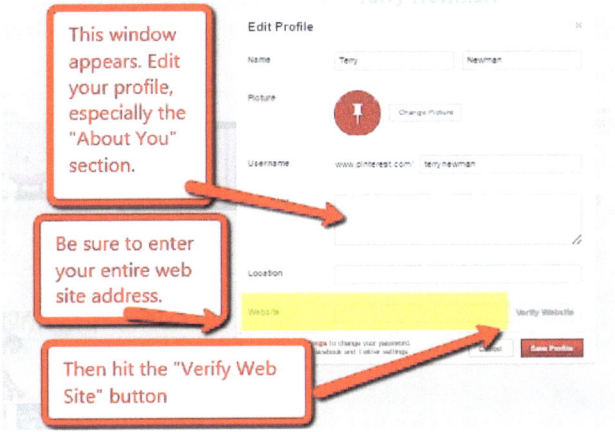

From there Pinterest will take you step-by-step through the short process. I

5. By all means, keep in active contact with individuals in the Pinterest community.

If you ask anyone in sales what the number one way to actually make the sale is, they'll tell you it's by first becoming the consumer's friend. The consumer wants to know that the bottom line is that you have her best interests at stake.

The same goes for Pinterest. And how do you do that? By staying active online, commenting on the boards of other users, repinning their images and photos, and in general just getting to know your customers and potential customers.

Use this same procedure whether you're selling furniture or life coaching services. Whether you're displaying your latest line of chaises or posting an inspirational quote, be sure you're in contact as much as possible with others. If someone comments on something you've posted, make a comment in return.

6. Avoid flooding your boards with self-promotion

Think about those emails you get in your box every day. You know which ones are going to be solely about buying this or that. Then there are those careful marketers who have a reputation for giving you some good information along with a sales pitch. Or perhaps they just offer the newest advances in their fields without that hard sell approach. Which ones do you continue to open? Exactly.

Not every post, image, or text from your Pinterest boards need to be about promoting your business. Tips on keeping furniture looking like new would be appropriate for furniture sellers along with an occasional sales pitch. Perhaps even some information about different types of woods or fabrics.

I was once told that about only 20% of what you post should be directly related to getting the sale. The other 80% should just be about spreading tips, observations, and inspirational photos. Try it, and see if it doesn't work for you.

7. Sponsor a Pinterest Contest

Why not? You could go about this in several ways and create a small gift certificate or another type of prize for the winner of the contest. For example, I've seen several "Pin to Win" contests. You challenge the general Pinterest community to create some interesting boards from your Pinterest site. Award a series of predetermined prizes for the most winners. A contest is a good way to create content among your followers with the added benefits of receiving links back to your site and product pages.

Type "Pin it to Win It Contests" into the search bar on your Pinterest home page and this window appears.

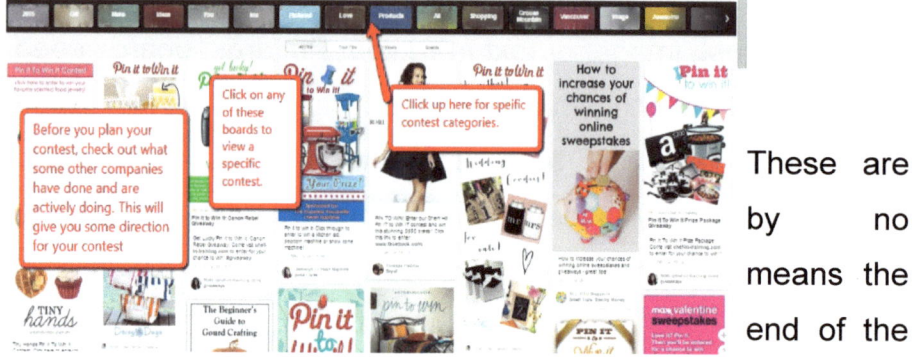

These are by no means the end of the marketing tips and techniques you can use to increase your business' presence on Pinterest. But they certainly will get you started – the rest is up to you.

CONCLUSION

The growing popularity of Pinterest is staggering. It's common for a new social media site to pop up and gain a large following rapidly, but the true test of any site is not only sustaining that user base but growing it.

The interest in Pinterest doesn't seem to be ebbing in the least. More people than ever before are joining and enjoying it every day.

One of the reasons for the rapid growth and the loyalty of its community is its ease of use. The creators of this site have made it as user friendly as possible and have provided you with plenty of encouragement. It's difficult to ask much more from any site.

Many individuals are using Facebook, for example, less. Some are upset about the growing appearance of advertising or being forced to pay for promotional plugs and "advertising" like posts that previously were free.

Other individuals are finding it exceedingly difficult to navigate the Facebook terrain. Some aren't visiting the site as frequently as they once were. Still others are drained of the "drama" that finds its way to the Facebook walls.

Private arguments easily become public knowledge and everybody and their brother are suddenly adding their opinions into mix. If some people are visiting the site less, others are actually deleting their accounts. You'll seldom find much drama on the Pinterest site. It always seems to be a pleasant place to visit.

Pinterest? It just might be the Paradise of the Cyber World.

www.ingramcontent.com/pod-product-compliance
Lightning Source LLC
Chambersburg PA
CBHW050824290526
45792CB00001B/254